by Van Nostrand Reinhold

s Catalog Card Number 88-15056

0-5

ong Kong

Monika Grejniec

and Reinhold
Avenue
, New York 10003

strand Reinhold (International) Limited
Fetter Lane
EC4P 4EE, England

ostrand Reinhold
La Trobe Street
ourne, Victoria 3000, Australia

cmillan of Canada
vision of Canada Publishing Corporation
4 Commander Boulevard
gincourt, Ontario M1S 3C7, Canada

16   15   14   13   12   11   10   9   8   7   6   5   4   3   2   1

Library of Congress Cataloging in Publication Data

Ladau, Robert F.
   Color in interior design and architecture / Robert F. Ladau, Brent K.
Smith, Jennifer Place.
      p.   cm.
   Bibliography: p.
   Includes index.
   ISBN 0-442-25830-5
   1. Color in interior design—Case studies.   2. Interior
architecture—Case studies.   I. Smith, Brent.   II. Place, Jennifer.
III. Title.
NK2115.5.C6L34   1988   88-15056
729—dc19   CIP

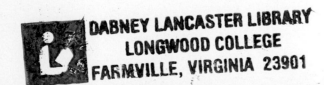

D0847787

CO

in Interior D

Robert F. Ladau   Brent K. S

Copyright © 1989

Library of Congre

ISBN 0-442-258

Printed in H

Designed by

Van Nostr
115 Fifth
New Yor

Van No
11 New
Londo

Van
480
Mel

Ma
Di
10
A

VNR Van Nostrand Reinhold
_____ New York

CONTENTS

ACKNOWLEDGMENTS

The authors wish to thank the following people for their contributions to this book: Mr. and Mrs. S. J. Miller, Roger Seifter, David Donihue at the Alternative Museum, Shellee Gero at Pantone, Bridgit Leicester, Dorothy Spencer, Janice Gehlmeyer, Sarah Bodine, Susan Schwartzenberg at the Exploratorium, Curt Roginson at Welton Beckett, and Pam Stein at Walker Group/CNI.

At Van Nostrand Reinhold, we would like to thank Lilly Kaufman and Paul Lukas for their invaluable help.

In addition, our thanks to all the architects, designers and photographers who contributed their work: Peter Aaron, Anthony Albarello, Ruth Ameil, Otto Baitz, Harold Corsini, Ambrose Cucinotta, James D'Addio, Jeff Greene, Scott Frances, Elliott Kaufman, Cork Marchesschi, Norman McGrath, Charles Moore, Charles Morris Mount, Peter Paige, Richard Payne, the Pratt Architectural Resource Center, Marvin Rand, Frank Ritter, Mark Ross, H. Durstan Saylor, Robert A. M. Stern, Horst Thanhauser, John Wadsworth, Walker Group/CNI, Ingrid Wagner, Welton Becket Assoc., Toshi Yoshimi, and Kate Zari.

Color has served as a decorative element on buildings from ancient times, as camouflage or as a contrasting element to the surrounding landscape. Photos: Sarah Bodine.

INTRODUCTION

Imagine an environment without color, an environment made up of solids and voids, edges and planes, soft and hard objects, textures and smooth surfaces. This environment would have function, attitude, and purpose. It would include every aspect of good design except one: color. Could that environment be considered a suitable place for human habitation?

Color is an integral part of the world we live in. But just because color exists all around us does not mean that it cannot be manipulated. Color can be natural or artificial, permanent or transitory, used for effect or emotion.

Color can also be a very powerful design tool, one that is capable of altering the perception or use of a space. Where form alone

once was used to create spatial interest, and materials or paint provided areas of color, now color itself is emerging as a way to define form and give a sense of scale. When space, material, or budget constraints all prove to be confinements on a project, using color effectively can, in many cases, solve design problems. When drama, architectural focus, or illusion is a desirable effect in a space, color can be the means to create it.

A designer can think about color in two ways: as design or as decoration. Color as design modifies or defines form. It can express history, shape or deepen space, add density, define edges, turn corners. Color as a design element cannot be formulaic. It does not use color in specific terms (red, blue, or yellow) but rather in terms of what different tonal contrasts can do to change a space.

Color used as decoration employs specific colors to create style. For example, it might deal with a specific fabric that could be enhanced by a particular wall color. Color as decoration uses aspects of history to recreate a feeling. It finds the metaphors in color and provides impact.

The aim of this book is to help the designer strike a balance between color used as design and color used as decoration. The goal is to be able to move skillfully back and forth between the two uses.

Approaching color is a matter of thought before action. It is essential to begin with concepts, then work toward solutions. The first section of this book will demonstrate quickly, through a series of photographs, some of color's potential, how it can modify the elements in a space. The next section provides the background: how light becomes

color and how we perceive color. We have not set out to write a book on physical science; this has been done very well in some of the books listed in the bibliography. Rather, we would like to give the designer a working vocabulary based on the science of color and light, and, most important, a visual understanding of the physical properties of the conditions that must be worked with in the design field.

The third section offers a brief overview of how color has been used in the history of design. It discusses the emotional impact of some of the key individual colors and also shows how color has been used effectively in clinical situations. Some discussion of the traditional rules for color use and the standard formulas for color schemes prepares the reader to proceed to the next section, which provides an innovative and flexible vocabulary for using color and talking about color.

The fourth section is the key to understanding how to think about color as a design tool. The discussion focuses on and develops six categories that break color down into manageable elements, which can then be applied to actual design situations.

The fifth section applies the color elements to actual case studies in which color has been used as a primary component of design. These case studies explore a wide variety of projects, from commercial to residential, from office to store, from historic to modern.

As you move back and forth between the sections of the book, it will become clear that color is much more than a passive attribute. It should be used as a design tool—in the same way as form or materials.

Color is evident in the natural surroundings as well as in the painted finishes of the building.
Photo: Brent K. Smith.

Chapter 1

THE COLOR CONDITION

Color can be warm or cool, rich or subtle, soft or hard. There are monochromatic, bichromatic, and trichromatic color schemes. Colors can be homogeneous or contrasting, pure or diffused. There are historic colors and new colors, projected colors and reflected colors. These are some of the various "conditions" that color can produce.

We are conditioned through culture and history to respond to color in a particular way, and it can take years for the eye and mind to adjust to unaccustomed color juxtapositions. New ways of using color are always slightly shocking even though they may be visually exciting.

The visual experience of color can be as diverse as color itself. The photographs that follow are a small demonstration of how color can shift our sensory perceptions, influence our emotions, and shape space.

NEW COLOR

A fabric showroom must "change its stripes" every season, presenting the latest colors and patterns. At the Designtex showroom in Washington, D.C., this sumptuous display of new colors is echoed by the reflective surfaces of the walls and ceiling and by the neon lighting. As light is bounced back and forth, the space seems to explode. High-contrast juxtapositions reinforce the function of the space, providing a clear case of design through color. Architect/Designer: Charles Morris Mount, New York City. Photo: Norman McGrath.

HISTORIC COLOR

The Royal Chapel at Versailles is a good example of how throughout history architects have relied on the inherent colors of natural materials to provide form. A lavish use of marble and gilt allowed the natural light and/or candlelight to reflect to maximum effect. There are no false surfaces. Applied colors are seen only in narrative paintings such as on the ceiling. The architectural forms and high-contrast colors reinforce the ceremonial aspets of this space, which might be seen as a tribute to spirit and light. Photo: Robert F. Ladau.

IDENTIFYING COLOR

This Chinese temple is immediately identifiable as Oriental by both its architecture and its color. If we could imagine these same colors on a different architectural form, the colors would still be unquestionably Oriental. It is the particular shades of each color in juxtaposition to each other that prompt our associations. Red is a symbol of joy in the Orient; here the symbolic use of color is as strong as its use as form or shape. Photo: Ruth Amiel.

ILLUSIONARY COLOR

These forms are painted on a flat surface. The sense of depth and scale are created rather than real. Everything depicted on the wall is an illusion, providing elegance and ornamentalism to what once was an ordinary commercial building now upgraded to condominiums. The colors are natural, painted a shade darker than desired to take into account fading and weathering. Designed by Evergreene P.S. Inc., New York City. Photo: Jeff Greene.

CONTRASTING COLOR

Dark against light; red against green; both of these elements are used in an eclectic room setting and help to turn it into a unified whole. A range of architectural references are harmoniously joined by the strength of the light/dark relationships. The green could be any dark color just so the strength remained the same. The diverse furnishings are related through light and dark contrast as well as through color contrast. Architect/Designer: Robert A. M. Stern, New York City. Photo: Horst Thanhauser.

HARD COLORS

The entrance to National Place in Washington D.C. draws the attention through the use of edges, crisp shadows, sharp contrasts, and brilliant white light. Although the colors are warm, they are hardened by the raw, exposed shapes and surfaces. The drama and lack of subtlety of the architecture guides the visitor toward the entrance, which explodes from the building out into the street. Architect/Designer: Walker Group/CNI, New York City. Photo: Mark Ross.

SOFT COLORS

Once inside National Place, the same colors that appeared on the exterior are mellowed through the use of soft materials and soft lighting. The basic cream neutrals are echoed by the soft pastel banners that are layered and draped from the ceiling. These banners delicately break up an otherwise big and bold space, at the same time providing a sense of movement through it by means of rhythmic color progressions. Architect/Designer: Walker Group/CNI, New York City. Photo: Mark Ross.

MONOCHROMATIC COLORS

A narrow range of colors makes up a monochromatic theme, shown here through a group of beiges and browns in a tapestry detail. Although the colors are few in number, the way in which the light hits the surface causes each one to lighten and darken, breaking up into further tints and shades of the original color. Tapestry and photo: Ruth Amiel.

REFLECTED COLOR

The Tropicana nightclub provides extreme dramatic effect by using a single color in a large space. The color functions as background to the stage. The rich red reflects onto all other surfaces (as well as onto the customers), unifying the entire space. The deep, flat tones are absorptive and make the lighting in the room supplementary, providing a dense, dark environment when the show is on. The color is pure theater. Architect/Designer: Welton Becket Associates, New York City. Photo: Anthony Alvarello.

RICH COLOR

In contrast to the Tropicana, the Opera House at Versailles, which is an even more lavish stage setting, is composed of natural materials instead of applied color. The result still reflects color and light throughout the space, but here the candles remained lighted during the opera and were given extra shimmer through the prisms. This is an intimidating and authentic space, that, while small in actual size, magnified the stature of its patron, Louis XIV. Photo: Robert F. Ladau.

ENERGIZING COLOR

The kinetic energy evident in this university café encourages reaction. The use of color and light is provocative and expressive. Form is created through light, and attention is drawn to the business at hand, eating and drinking, by the strong red of the tables. Architect: Charles Moore. Photo courtesy the Pratt Architecture Resource Center.

FOUND COLOR

Gaudi's use of found materials brings a fanciful, organic dimension to this fountain in Barcelona Park. The fractured colors are bright and strong, yet they convey naturalism because of the white areas breaking up the intensely colored areas. This provides shadows, just as colors are shadowed in nature. The placement of color is purely artistic expression, but the result is a rich ornamental use of color and an appropriate mix of rough surface and slick tile for a fountain. Architect: Antonio Gaudi. Photo courtesy the Pratt Architecture Resource Center.

THEATRICAL COLOR

A casino immediately reflects glamour and glitz. It is a kinetic, light-filled space that is designed to dissolve time and keep its clientele awake long into the night. Both the color and the lighting are highly dramatic. The deep reflective colors are rich, almost plush. The lighting provides infinite repetition and dazzle. This is an "all-American" environment, geared toward homogenizing and energizing its clients. Architect/Designer: Welton Becket Associates, New York City. Photo: Anthony Alvarello.

NATURAL COLOR

Colors in a garden naturally change because of the seasons. But if these colors are also controlled by design, they can provide a whole new range of contrasts and densities. Nature takes strong hues and shadows them; surfaces are never flat or unreflective. In this garden, the red and green contrast created by grass and flowers is further refined by the man-made edges of the garden design. Photo: Robert F. Ladau.

BICHROMATIC COLORS

A two-color theme can be composed of many variations and layers. Here, the wood tones of the seating area contrast with the blue-violet-pink lights in the rear. Both wood and light are reflective, and the play of light encourages each area to be much more dimensional than if flat or monochromatic colors had been used. The contrasts are mellow rather than strong, creating a restful atmosphere. Architect/Designer: Charles Morris Mount, New York City. Photo: Elliott Kaufman.

CULTURAL COLORS

This guesthouse could be part of any American family's domain. It shows the passage of time and the accumulation of a life of gathering eclectic bits and pieces. Its colors are warm, integral, and unplanned, yet culturally evocative. Time and place are not specific, but the overall effect is one that represents a particular way of living. Photo courtesy Ruth Amiel.

AMBIENT LIGHT/COLOR

The neutral color in this room enables the natural light to function as a strong design element. The light is drawn into the deep room and reflects off the warm off-white and pink tones, creating an ambient light that mellows the sharp architectural forms by negating the shadows. Architect/Designer: Robert A. M. Stern, New York City. Photo: Peter Aaron.

TRICHROMATIC COLOR

Red, yellow, and blue and their variations are used to recall historic color and form. A flat, absorptive patina creates the "idea" that this space has been here for a long time, yet the architectural forms are very modern versions of classic themes. These colors reflect in much the same way as if they were opulent materials, recreating marble and stone through *trompe l'oeil*. The colors honor the past and provide a sense of importance. Architect/Designer: Charles Morris Mount, New York City. Photo: Scott Frances.

Color is light. Photo: Brent K. Smith.

Chapter 2

THE SCIENCE OF COLOR

Color is shattered light. In order to use color it is important to know something about how light becomes color. This process and its vocabulary are the key to actually using color.

This section will explore how light becomes color through dispersion, diffraction, interference, reflection, and absorption. It will show how we optically perceive color and how we respond to its various characteristics. We will discuss how reflected light and color and projected light and color combine in various ways to make up the majority of situations that color our world. We will define the working vocabulary of color: pigments, hues, tints, and shades and contrasts. Finally, this section will explore the differences between natural and artificial light and how each one will change our perception of color.

LIGHT

Color is light and light is one of the known forms of radiant energy.

Visible light, which is responsible for color, is a narrow band of the electromagnetic spectrum that falls between ultraviolet

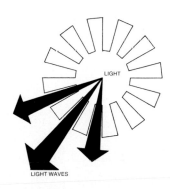

Light emanates from the sun.

and infrared light. Other known electromagnetic radiations include radio waves, x-rays, gamma rays, and cosmic rays. The small interval of the spectrum that contains visible light is given to us as sunlight, which is white or uncolored light, and contains all the spectral colors: red, orange, yellow, green, blue, indigo, and violet.

Light travels in predictable and measurable patterns. The most well-known theory is that light travels in an undulating wave-like motion. These wavelengths vibrate at different frequencies, and the number of frequencies of vibration determine the individual colors. Red has the lowest number of vibrations (430,000 times in a billionth of a second); violet the highest (732,000 times).

The small band of the electromagnetic spectrum that is visible light is given to us in the form of sunlight. Photo: Janice Gehlmeyer.

A further refinement of the wavelength theory of how light travels is the quantum theory, which proposes that the waves of light exist as chunks, or quanta, that travel as streams of particles, or photons. Photons, made up of atoms with varying structures, gain and lose energy in varying amounts, therefore producing different colors. While the energy level of the photons determines the color of the light, the number of photons determines the intensity of light.

White light, or sunlight, does not automatically separate into different colors. Rather, the emanating wavelengths must be interrupted in some way before they will break up into colors that can then be perceived by our eyes and brain.

COLOR

Color is essentially a refinement of light. In the absence of light all objects appear to be colorless, existing as shades of neutral gray.

A full range of white light, or 3500 Kelvin, contains each color of the spectrum—red, orange, yellow, green, blue, indigo, violet—in full intensity. None of these colors exists, however, until the light waves are interrupted and reflected, enabling our eyes to perceive this information and transmit it to the brain. Light waves can be interrupted in several ways.

Dispersion

Color can be perceived through dispersion, which is what happens when light is passed through a prism (a transparent optical device having nonparallel, flat surfaces). In 1676 Sir Isaac Newton discovered that when sunlight is passed through a prism the light is bent, or refracted, resulting in an ordered display of individual colors. The arrangement of these colors is always the same, from the longest wavelengths (red) to the shortest (violet), with orange, yellow, green, blue, and indigo falling between the two extremes. The shorter the wavelength, the greater the refraction, and vice versa. Between each of the spectral colors refracted through a prism are infinite gradations that are both difficult to detect and without specific names.

Nature provides a look at spectral color through the rainbow, which occurs when sunlight passes through raindrops, is refracted, and reflected back. Rainbows provide distinct bands of red, orange, yellow, yellow green, green, blue green, blue, violet, and purple.

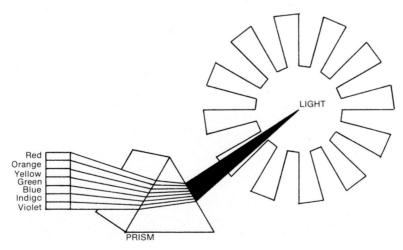

A prism breaks light into its component colors.

When light passes through a prism or a multifaceted transparent structure, as shown in this *crystal light painting* by Ingrid Wagner, it breaks up into spectral colors. Photo courtesy the Alternative Museum, New York City.

Diffraction

Light can also be broken up into colors through diffraction, which involves bending light by sending it through a very small slit or against very sharp edges. Peacock feathers and opal stones, each of which has tiny hard edges, are examples of color produced through diffraction.

When light is passed through a small slit, as in a crack in a doorway, it diffracts light into colors. Photo: Susan Schwartzenberg; courtesy the Exploratorium, Ca.

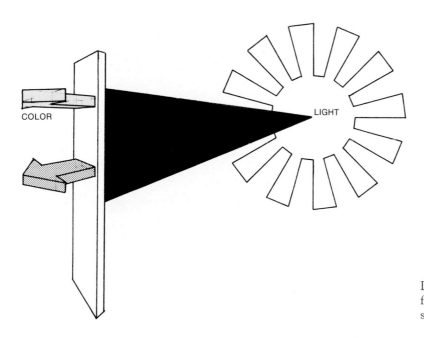

Diffraction produces color by forcing light through very small slits.

Interference

Color can occur when light passes through thin films, such as oil, that do not allow light waves to penetrate completely. Sunlight shining on deep water is refracted from the wave action on the surface, which produces shimmering bands of color at the bottom. Iridescence, the shimmering effect found on the surface of a drop of oil or in the wings of insects, forms when light waves are forced to interfere with each other constantly because of the layers in the structure of the object.

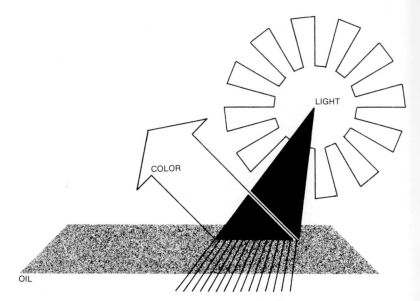

An oil film or other transparent medium produces color through interference.

Absorption/Reflection

The most common method of producing different colors is through absorption/reflection. When light hits an object, some of the light waves are absorbed by the molecules of the object's surface, while others are completely or partially reflected off the surface. These reflected light waves are picked up by our eyes and transmitted to the brain as color information. To appear red, for example, an object will absorb almost all of the spectral wavelengths except the reds, which will reflect.

Most of our world is colored by reflection and absorption. Color, therefore, is not an inherent property in an object. An orange is not orange, a grape is not green. They are colored by their particular molecular structure, which allows certain wavelengths of light to be absorbed into their surfaces and others to be reflected in order to be perceived by our eyes.

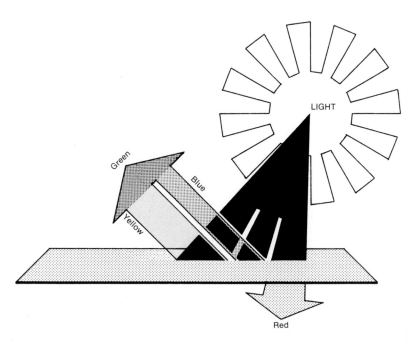

Color is produced when light hits a surface and is either absorbed or reflected by it.

THE PERCEPTION OF COLOR

Color does not exist without light. We do not actually see color until the light waves that enter the eye stimulate the receptive cones located in the back of the eye. This stimulation causes an electrical disturbance that is transferred to the optical nerves behind the eyeball and is in turn fed to the optical area at the base of the brain. The brain then turns this information into color.

Although the brain receives complete color information from light, it cannot analyze the various wavelengths individually in the same way the ear can interpret the notes in a chord. Instead, the cones in the eye are receptive to only three colors in the spectrum—red, blue, and yellow. These three colors appear distinct because each stimulates its receptor in a different way. Red,

blue, and yellow form the primary colors of the spectrum, and our eyes mix them to create all remaining colors. When combined equally, these three colors produce white, or colorless, light.

When the retina, the part of the eye that receives images, is hit with an image containing a particularly bright band of light, an interesting phenomenon called lateral inhibition occurs. The band of light will hit one part of the retina, making the rest of it less sensitive to light. The eye will therefore darken surrounding areas of the image, creating contrast and exaggerating edges. Light areas will look brighter; dark areas will deepen even further.

Historically, the most commonly held belief has been that color perception is the di-

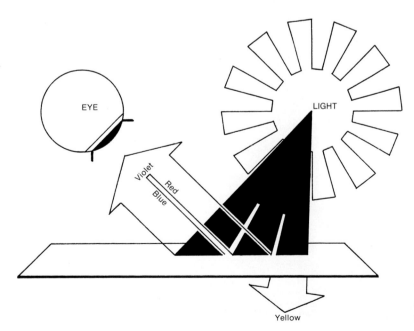

We perceive color through our eyes when it is reflected from a surface.

rect result of the reaction of the eye's color sensors (cones) to the redness, greenness, or the blueness of the light from an individual surface, independent of its surroundings.

Recent studies suggest, however, that color perception depends on the light from an individual surface as compared with the light reflected from surrounding surfaces. We know that the color of shadows, for example, are influenced by the reflected color of the object casting the shadow. The same shadow, however, also can be influenced by the reflected colors nearby. Our eyes do not discriminate and take in only the light from the object in particular focus. Color, therefore, is not at all a static condition.

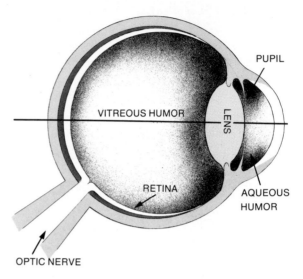

The parts of the eye.

REFLECTED LIGHT AND REFLECTED COLOR

While we know that most objects in the world are colored by reflection and absorption, subtle differences should be noted between the terms *reflected light* and *reflected color*.

Reflected light is light that has not been fully or partially absorbed by the surface of an object and hence "bounces" back to the viewer. This light is white, or colorless, light. When light shines on a smooth surface,

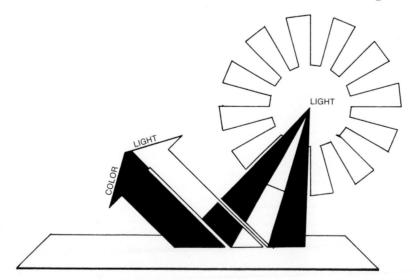

Reflected light joins with reflected color before it is perceived by the eye.

much of the light is reflected back. On a rough surface, the many different levels of the surface cause the light to reflect back in various directions.

Reflected color is how our eyes interpret the light reflected back from an object, or, those parts of the color spectrum that have not been fully absorbed. The white light that has not penetrated the surface at all mixes with the light reflected back from within the object and desaturates the depth or intensity of the color. Reflected color is rarely pure. Although a smooth surface may reflect a dominant color, it will usually be mixed with bits of the other colors of the spectrum as well. A rough surface reflects the same color, but it will appear less intense or duller.

A black object absorbs almost all the light coming to its surface; conversely, a white object reflects almost all light waves (snow, for example, or metal, which shines back so much it produces a mirror image). Just as we do not see truly "pure" colors, we do not see pure black or white either. Rather, we see various shades of black and white: coal black, blue-black, eggshell white, milky white, and so forth.

An object appears transparent when its molecular structure allows most of the light to pass through the object without being either absorbed or reflected. A thin surface layer will permit light to pass through it sufficiently to make the object quite transparent, like glass. As surface layers become thicker, however, a semi-transparent state will eventually be reached. Water, for example, will only allow light waves to penetrate to a certain depth before they are completely absorbed (hence the blackness at the bottom of a pond).

PROJECTED LIGHT AND PROJECTED COLOR

Man has devised a number of ways to recreate, enhance, and even alter, natural light, and therefore establish color.

One of these ways is to interfere with any projected light, sunlight, or artificial light, before it hits the surface of an object. Placing a filter between the light source and the object prevents some of the light waves from ever striking the surface, or to hit weakly, resulting in a distinct change in the reflected color. A beam of white light, when disturbed with a blue filter, will color any object it hits with a bluish tone. A yellow flower, hit with a blue light, will take on a greenish cast. This is projected color.

The theater takes full advantage of projected light techniques, creating scary or evil effects with greenish lights, making shadows overdramatic, enabling a bit of cloth and paint to turn into rolling landscape.

The mortal world uses projected light too. Artificial light, which will be discussed in more detail later, casts either a bluish or a yellowish tone and influences our perception of color accordingly. We have also learned to use projected light for subtle effects. It is

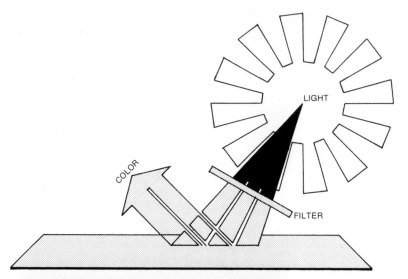

Interrupting projected light with a filter before it hits a surface changes the reflected color.

Light projected on an object, when colored by a filter or gel, will change the color of the object. Photos: Susan Schwartzenberg; courtesy the Exploratorium, Ca.

common practice to project a rosy pink light on patrons in a restaurant to create more flattering skin tones. In a supermarket the meat counter will often have reddish light to enhance the visual appeal of the product. A discotheque will make heavy use of neon lighting, because while neon creates color, it does not illuminate: rather, it glows. The energy is dispelled in the creation of the color.

PIGMENT

Light will not create color if it is not filtered through molecules that absorb and reflect the light waves.

This molecular structure is called a pigment, and it is responsible for the particular colors that will be perceived. It is the individual molecular vibrations that determine which light waves will be absorbed or reflected, hence determining color.

The term *pigment* can be used for both the natural source of color and for a manmade colorant. A green leaf, for example, has chlorophyll as a pigment, which absorbs all the wavelengths of spectral color except green. Other natural pigments include carotene, which accounts for many reds, yellows,

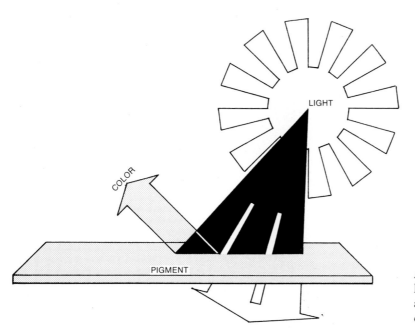

A pigment is either applied or inherent in the surface of an object and determines the colors that are either reflected or absorbed.

Natural pigments provide a wealth of intense and rich colors. Photo: Brent K. Smith.

and oranges found, especially in vegetables; melanin, which colors the skin; and hemoglobin, which colors the blood.

Man has long extracted elements from nature to use as applied colorants. Mineral pigments provide a wide range of color—zinc oxide, raw umber, and graphite are examples—as do many vegetal extracts—woods, barks, fruits, and grasses. In order for a mineral substance to be used as a pigment it must be thoroughly washed, pulverized, baked, and ground again before it can be added to a medium (oil, water, egg) and used. Vegetable pigments must be ground, cooked, and dried before use. Even animals provide pigment in the form of substances such as bones and shells. These pigments, however, have often proved unstable over time. Today, with the advent of synthetic pigments, color is not only stable, but the range of colors available is practically limitless. Synthetic pigments are derived from a large variety of organic and non-organic substances. Tar is one commonly used example, which when properly distilled yields very pure, intense, and long-lasting colors.

HUES

Each color of the spectrum has a single measurable vibration or frequency. True spectral colors do not occur in nature; rather, all natural colors are hues—two or more spectral colors observed simultaneously.

A hue, therefore, is a gradation or a variety of a color. About twenty-four hues of full intensity can be discerned by the eye, but there are an infinite number of gradations possible in between. In any color combination there is usually a dominant hue that enables a color to fit into a pure hue category, scarlet red, for example.

The term *chroma* is used to define a spectral color that has only one vibration. Chroma is a reflection of the purity of a color, or its freedom from white or gray.

Hues can be manipulated by adjusting the pigment on the surface of an object. Different ways of adjustment include combining hues, using opaque or transparent hues, or varying a hue by changing any of its qualifying factors: intensity, saturation, temperature, or value.

Intensity

Intensity describes the strength, brightness, or luminosity of a hue, which is the amount or intensity of light being projected or reflected. Bright colors are not necessarily pure colors, but the brightness of a hue can be manipulated by adding or subtracting the amount of white light allowed to affect the hue.

Temperature

Colors often are described in terms of temperature. The warmth or coolness of a color is a comparative condition. Basically, the reds, oranges, and yellows are warm; the blues, greens, and violets are cool. Beyond that, the temperature of a color is determined by a hue's additive rather than by the color itself. Thus, warm colors can be made cooler and cool colors warmer by adding colors from the opposite end of the spectrum. Reddish blue, for example, is warmer than greenish blue; reddish yellow is warmer than bluish red.

Saturation

Color saturation is the level of maximum chroma or purity, the degree of freedom from admixture of white. Chemically, this involves the strength of the colorant solution: a fully saturated color contains the maximum amount of pigment the color can handle. Red, for example, can be brilliant or pale depending on its saturation. Saturation can also be considered the degree of difference between the pure hue and its tint or shade.

TINTS AND SHADES

By adding or subtracting light from a saturated color you create a tint or a shade. Lightness, determined by how much light is reflected from a surface, is a color's degree of difference from black. A color's darkness, or lack of reflected light, is its closeness to black. This is also called a color's value.

A color can be altered either by varying the quantity of light allowed to reach the surface or by adding light or dark to the original pigment.

Adding more light, or white, to a color produces a *tint*. A limitless number of gradations can be produced between the saturated color and white.

Reducing the amount of light, or adding black, to a color, produces a *shade*. Again, very subtle gradations are possible within the scale from hue to black.

A shade of a color, however, can also be produced simply by lowering the light level in a room with a rheostat. A neutral-density filter (a filter that uniformly reduces light without color bias) can also be used to affect color to produce tints and shades.

CONTRAST

Contrast expresses differences between colors. There are many types of contrasts, in-cluding light and dark, black and white, and warm and cool.

Light and Dark Contrasts

Light and dark contrast can refer to either the amount of light hitting a surface or the actual value of a color. The farther apart two colors are on a black-and-white scale, the more contrast there is between them.

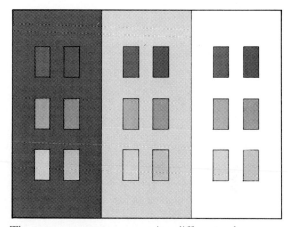

The same tones appear quite different when contrasted against a light, medium, and a dark tone.

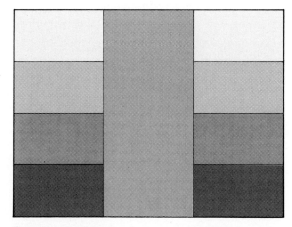

Contrast of value.

Warm and Cool Contrast

Warm and cool colors can provide a sense of temperature contrast. They will clash and can be uncomfortable to look at side by side. A cool color placed next to a warm color (blue-red next to orange-red, for example), will not be harmonious.

Complementary Contrast

Contrast is most often used, however, to describe color opposites, or complementary colors. When pure light hits a surface, is absorbed or reflected, and is translated into color, only a specific portion of the spectrum is revealed in that color. The remaining colors in the spectrum are "left over." It is these colors, combined, that form the contrasting color to the reflected hue. For example, when light hits a red surface, blue and yellow are absorbed and red is reflected. Blue and yellow combine to make green, which is the complementary contrast of red and directly opposite on the color wheel.

Mixed together, complementary colors form a neutral gray-black. Side by side, complementary colors set up the maximum amount of contrast between two colors and will cause a visual vibration. In painting it is usual to shade a color with its complement.

Simultaneous Contrast

Any two colors placed side by side provide simultaneous contrast and will affect one another. Gray placed next to blue will make the blue appear yellowish. Complementary colors have maximum contrast, and when they are placed side by side the sense of contrast between them will be enhanced. Identical colors, when viewed against different backgrounds, will appear slightly different to the eye.

Other Types of Contrast

It is also possible to explore contrast in terms of saturation, or how much of each color a hue might contain. Two colors that make a whole, for example, a color composed of 80 percent red and 20 percent green, would contrast with a color of opposite proportions. Successive contrast occurs when a complementary afterimage is produced by staring at a color, then quickly looking at a white area.

The concept of contrast can be taken even further by considering the following: transparent/opaque, smooth/rough, light/heavy, straight/curved, or thick/thin. Color can be affected by each of these contrasting conditions

Contrast can be an effective tool in design, in terms of both color and texture. While too much contrast might be irritating, a certain amount can create visual excitement.

NATURAL LIGHT

The light of day, dictated by the rising and setting of the sun, is an ever-changing condition that affects how we see color. Natural light changes from dawn to dusk and from season to season, depending on the positions of the earth and sun. The intensity of light changes according to longitude and latitude as well as weather conditions.

Dawn brings light but little color, making everything appear cool and gray. Once the sun rises color gradually warms, peaking at midday when the sun gives off its most intense white light, deepening shadows and intensifying color. In the afternoon the light becomes warmer still, turning everything a rosy gold as sunset nears. Clouds, at any time of the day, filter the red, orange, and yellow light waves, dulling color.

For purposes of standardization, color is considered truest when viewed under conditions of the strongest daylight. Under this standard, light colors appear intense and clean. Shadows appear short and dark, emphasizing the contrasts between hues. It is common practice to take a possible purchase into bright daylight to check its "true" colors.

Natural light affects the colors in the interior as well as the exterior of a space. Walls, furniture, and fabrics are all influenced by the light at different times of day. Rooms facing east will be washed with bright morning light; those facing west will bask in the warmer afternoon light. Northern light, so prized by artists for their studios, is bright but cool. Because this light contains all the spectral colors, it offers ac-

Natural light affects color at various times of day. Photo: Janice Gehlmeyer.

curate color matching for the artist. Colors will appear brighter when struck directly with light, and will seem more muted when tucked into the shadows. Skylights give diffused overall light. Designers either can take advantage of natural lighting conditions or can attempt to counterbalance their effects.

ARTIFICIAL LIGHT

With modern technology light can do much more than just illuminate. Artificial light can lighten, darken, warm, cool, brighten, flat-ten, or entirely change a color. In addition, man-made sources of light have limited ranges of spectral color and hence can change the color/light absorption level of the surfaces in a room. If a color is not contained in the light source to begin with, it will not appear in the surrounding areas.

From his earliest days man has found methods of providing light when natural light was absent. Most varieties of artificial lighting are produced by creating some form of heat, as the development of non-natural sources shows: from firelight, man went on to animal/vegetable oil light, candles, petroleum oil lamps, and then to gas, carbon in-

Artificial light was developed to provide illumination in the absence of natural light. Photo: Janice Gehlmeyer.

Neon is a decorative form of artificial light that emits a soft glow rather than a strong light.
Photo: Janice Gehlmeyer.

candescent, tungsten, fluorescent, neon, sodium vapor, metal halide, and laser lighting. Our most common methods of lighting today are incandescent and fluorescent.

Incandescent light, commonly used in domestic lighting, is produced by passing a current through a filament in a vacuum. A vacuum will not support combustion, so the light glows. The normal incandescent bulb is warm and slightly yellower than daylight, but colored bulbs such as blue or pink are also available.

Fluorescence is the emission of radiation by a substance during exposure to external radiation. Fluorescent lighting consists of a tube of inert gas with electrodes on either end of the tube. As electricity passes through the tube it activates a fluorescent coating on the inside of the tube, which gives off a glow. Fluorescent lights tend to be cold and flat, throwing few shadows and offering no highlights. Fluorescent bulbs come in many colors and can also be made to simulate sunlight for growing plants or to duplicate northern light. The color of a fluorescent bulb is determined by the particular gas selected or by the type of coating used on the inside of the tube.

Neon is similar to fluorescent lighting in that inert gases are used to produce colors, but the light from a neon bulb has very little focus and travels almost no distance at all. It is useful for dramatic effect, in a nightclub, for example, where little task lighting is needed.

Metal halide bulbs include quartz halogen, sodium vapor, quartz iodide, and tungsten halogen. These are high-voltage bulbs that burn a filament in an inert gas chamber. They produce extremely intense light that is difficult to control and creates a great deal of color distortion. Halogen bulbs also have a tendency to explode because of inside pressure and "hot spots." Most require some sort of protective shield. Car headlights are made with halogen bulbs, as are the street lamps that emit a very orange glow. Sodium-vapor lamps are so intense that they cannot be used in parks because they keep the trees "awake." Halogen bulbs do, however, lend themselves to innumerable design treatments because of their small size and high intensity. Innovative treatment has now brought the halogen bulb into the home as well as to industry.

Laser light is useful for the scientific community but of little use to the built environment, as prolonged exposure to this type of light produces harmful effects. Its concentrated beam of light, amplified by a stimulated emission of radiation, is so pure that it will emerge from a prism exactly as it entered it.

MEASURING LIGHT

The intensity of light is measured in foot candles: one foot candle is the illumination produced by one candle at a distance of one foot and equal to one lumen incident per square foot. The number of foot candles produced by a particular type of lighting, plus the reflection level of painted or other room surfaces, can give a designer a great deal of information about how to light a space.

The whitest outdoor light has a color rendering index (CRI) of 100 and a color temperature of 3500K. This reflects how a light's spectral distribution will render the color of an object. A cool white fluorescent bulb, for example, has a CRI of 68 and a temperature of 4200K. Below 3500K, light is more yellow; above that temperature it is more blue.

USING LIGHT

Color cannot exist if it is not in the light source. Ideally, artificial light should come as close as possible to white, outdoor light in quantity and intensity. But this does not take into account economics or mood. Any artificial light offers some amount of color that will affect its surroundings. How much, and to what effect, are what makes designing with a combination of light and color so interesting.

In the business world lighting is often controlled by a mixture of economics and necessity. Incandescent light creates warmth and ambience, but it is costly and it is difficult to get enough light into a large space. Fluorescent lighting is much cheaper to use but can seem cold and harsh in a large space. A combination of the two might be the answer, using incandescent lamps for drama and fluorescent cove lighting around the perimeter of the room for strength. Today's offices need specialized lighting treatments, to avoid glare in an area of computer terminals, for example.

Artificial light can also be controlled by numerous devices such as dimmers, framing projectors, lenses, and filters, all of which alter the intensity or control the direction of light.

LIGHT AND SURFACE

When considering lighting it is also important to take into consideration the surface the light will hit, whether it is shiny, matte, soft, hard, irregular, or smooth. A highly polished surface will reflect 75 to 95 percent of the light that hits it and absorb very little. A surface that is very light in color will also absorb little light. White paper, for example, absorbs about 18 percent of the light it receives; newsprint, on the other hand, absorbs about 40 percent. Pale colors will absorb from 30 to 60 percent of the light;

darker colors, from 60 percent up. Matte surfaces will absorb more light than shiny ones, and irregular surfaces will send the reflected light back in many directions.

LIGHT AND COLOR

The color of light affects the color of surface, and the quantity of light determines the quantity of reflected color. Bluish-white walls combined with very yellow incandescent light, for example, will appear slightly green. A lack of light darkens color, while an addition of light intensifies color. For example, a warm pink bulb placed over a dining area creates a flattering setting. A designer can recreate the feeling of candlelight in a period room or provide sunlight in a windowless space. Low, diffused light can be used to combat stress in an office situation light can add intense drama to a display or to a restaurant with hot spotlights. The combinations and possibilities are infinite.

THE EFFECTS OF COLOR AND LIGHT

Nature provides us with sunlight and a large variety of reflected hues. Our technology has given us artificial light and an ability to create an unlimited palette of hues as well as to duplicate pure spectral colors. All of these kinds of light can be manipulated by a designer to create particular effects. The three elements to keep in mind are light, color, and surface.

Light

Projected light imposes a filter between a light source and a surface. A red-colored gel can be placed over a spotlight directed on a yellow chair, and the object will certainly look orange. Reflected light imposes a "filter" on the surface of an object, generally as a pigment. A chair covered in orange fabric,

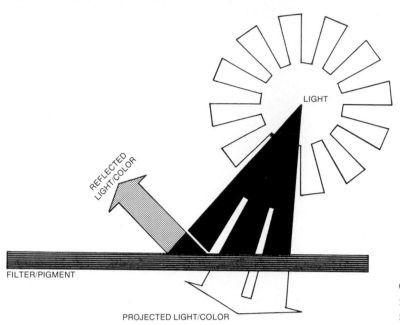

LIGHT

REFLECTED LIGHT/COLOR

FILTER/PIGMENT

PROJECTED LIGHT/COLOR

Combining projected and reflected light and color yields infinite color possibilities.

for example, can be made warmer or rosier by using a warm light in the room.

The brightness of light can also completely change the effects of color. The amount of light hitting a surface determines the amount of light reflected, and hence the brightness of the color.

Each element in a room can be controlled independently through reflected light and color combined with projected light and color. Combining these elements in varying degrees produces an unlimited palette.

Color

The intrinsic qualities of color offer effects that can be used to alter the perception of a space or of an object in a space.

Take, for example, red and blue. In normal light, red, with its longer wavelengths, has a tendency to appear close. Blue, with

its shorter wavelengths, recedes. In the fading light of evening, however, this situation is reversed. Red will fade, and blue will be the last color visible before all colors disappear.

Intense colors appear to come forward. Yellow, especially, seems to expand, while

COLOR OF OBJECT	APPEARANCE UNDER			
	Red Light	Blue Light	Yellow Light	Green Light
RED	RED	VIOLET	ORANGE	BROWN
YELLOW	ORANGE	GREEN	YELLOW	YELLOW GREEN
GREEN	DARK RED	BLUE GREEN	YELLOW GREEN	GREEN
PALE BLUE	VIOLET	BLUE	GREEN	BLUE GREEN

Some examples of how colors change under various projected colors.

Colors change dramatically from one season to the next in nature. Photos courtesy Robert F. Ladau.

other colors, such as violet, tend to contract. Light or grayed colors also recede. A dark object will usually look smaller than a light object of equal size.

Surface

The surface on which color is applied will also affect the look of the color. A rough texture or a deep pile carpet will darken color by absorbing more light and providing shadows. Matte or medium-textured fabrics also have low light reflection. A smooth surface, however, will reflect more light and color will seem truer. Highly reflective or shiny surfaces will also alter color appearance, especially where the light hits the surface.

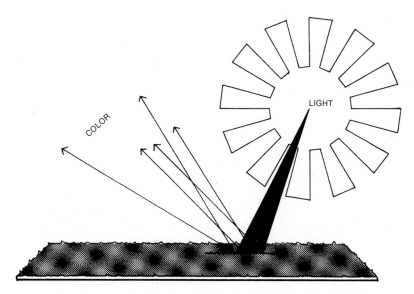

When color bounces off an irregular surface it is more diffused than if deflected from a smooth surface.

THE COLOR/LIGHT EQUATION

When working with color it is essential to remember that both the actual pigment and the light reaching the pigment must be kept in balance. The amount of light reflected from a surface can have as much to do with a color effect as the components of a pigment. The reflection level can be both measured and controlled, creating more intense or more subtle color.

Mistakes commonly occur in the color/light equation under the following conditions:

1. The right color but the wrong intensity,

2. The right color but the wrong reflection level,

3. The right level of intensity but the wrong type of lighting.

A yellow room designed to create an effect of warm sunlight will not work if the yellow chosen is a pale lemon color (an example of the first condition). A bright red chair will not look bright red if it is placed in a dark corner (an example of the second condition). The most common mistake is to use the wrong type of lighting. Warm white lightbulbs will cause a green color scheme to go putty gray, for example, and will make people in the room look a bit seasick. It is important to remember that light from artificial sources is either warm (red), cool (blue), or daylight (yellow).

Color has been used as a decorative application in design since earliest times. Here, bright blue enhances a Russian monastery. Photo: Sarah Bodine.

Chapter 3

COLOR IN DESIGN

Man has attempted to use color to suit his own needs since before the beginning of history. In earliest times, although it was not scientifically understood, color was given religious and symbolic qualities and used widely for personal and environmental decoration.

The history of color in design parallels the sociological and political climate of the times. The following section will provide an overview of this history before delving into the more specific complexities of color identity and color classification—from the color wheel to the modern day color scheme. The section also includes a discussion of how color is used in institutional settings, where it is chosen for its effect on personality and behavior rather than for its decorative properties. Understanding how color has been used in past design is necessary preparation for the subsequent section, which introduces a vocabulary of color use that can be applied to any environmental setting.

A SHORT HISTORY OF COLOR IN DESIGN

The use of color in design has evolved over the centuries, influenced by both necessity and availability. Man's instinct to decorate himself and his environment has spurred creative color use as far back as prehistoric times.

Color was a natural part of life for early man. Dyes made from blood, earth, fruits, and vegetables colored both the body and the walls of caves. Body painting decorated the color of the flesh. Wall painting mimicked nature through the use of color and symbolic figures. The earliest colors available were red, white, and black. Throughout history these colors have been associated with rituals and magic, bridging the gap between the physical and the metaphysical worlds.

As man evolved, colored pigments became important and more readily available. The use of color remained tied to religious symbolism. For the Egyptians gold was the

In this tapestry it is obvious that color as well as form is strongly Oriental. Photo courtesy Ruth Ameil.

color of sunlight and of creation. Colors also came to designate various gods. To the Greeks and the Romans, colors were extensions of the natural colors found in the Mediterranean world and were therefore strong and intense. During the age of Pericles color was thought to have symbolized mixtures of sun, fire, air, and water.

In medieval times principles associated with herbal medicine, alchemy, and the metaphysical world carried over into color, giving particular colors meaning beyond decoration. During the Renaissance painterly concepts changed from flat and diagramatic to shadowed and dimensional, and this brought neutral tones as well as perspective to the arts. It is interesting to note that opulent color and decoration have always been used for their own sake to identify wealth and stature.

In northern Europe colors were more subdued in keeping with the landscape. Colors reflected natural materials—wood, stone, and marble—which tended to restrict the decorative palette despite the increased number of paint colorants available. Walls were covered in dark fabrics as protection from the effects of weather.

Through the Renaissance and even into the 1800s, color was an idea steeped in the metaphysical or in nature, but was far removed from the manipulative color schemes we use today. The science of mixing colors had not matured, dyes were still unstable and unavailable, and fabrics and materials were limited. Before the eighteenth century, the French thought of color as a personal "coat of arms" or as insignia for status. Each reign would usher in a new profusion of colors and styles that would identify its time and place. Important religious figures also attached status to colors, as in their use of rich red and purple robes. Color was also used to identify particular religious holidays (the somber purple worn during Lent, for example). Textiles became more and more lavish and furnishings more and more decorative.

The baroque and rococo styles mixed pastels with elaborate brocades and a liberal use of gold and silver. The English style of this period was slightly more subdued than the French, using darker values and simpler forms.

The nineteenth century introduced true color schemes, and each of the prevalent styles—Victorian, Directoire, Sheridan, Georgian—had its prerequisite groups of colors that dictated its identity. The Victorians, for example, favored deep, rich reds and greens as well as mauves and browns. These color schemes were balanced; every warm color against a cool opposite color. In addition, the colors were used in relation to pattern and therefore provided scale. Weaving became more sophisticated, making fabric more available, so that it covered walls, floors, and furniture. Fabric motifs were still based in nature.

The twentieth century brought a strong reaction to the dark corridors of Victorian homes. New technology and many more dyes provided more colors. Central heating eliminated the need for heavy wall coverings. This modernist ideology permitted a new approach to color and form. Colors became light and free; form became streamlined and dynamic.

The Art Deco and Art Nouveau movements in the early part of the century saw color as a graphic solution and used clean, single color themes to support organic form. Colors such as peach and pale green decorated the exotic woods of the furnishings. Black-and-white tiles were used on floors.

Around World War I, intense colors based on Oriental themes or on the paintings of the Fauves gave rooms the look of theater or of costume.

During the 1920s the Bauhaus design philosophy, based on an industrial/machine aesthetic rather than on a natural one, was quick to counter all this color, however, and for the first time designers thought about what color could do to form rather than which specific colors to use as decoration. Bauhaus adherents found that only a minimum number of colors—the primary colors, black, white, and gray—were needed to make form stand out, space turn, twist, lighten, or darken. These colors were also easy to mass-produce, did away with difficult color choices and fussy custom color matching, and were to influence design and decoration for many years.

From the Depression through World War II, color became subdued due to economic reasons and the rationing of dyes, and also because the nation's technology was focused on the war effort. Color reflected the mood of the times.

The 1930s brought the softer all-white room as well as a combination of neutrals used as a theme in response to the machine aesthetic of the Bauhaus. At the same time, Frank Lloyd Wright was designing his organic houses, which used neutral tones to complement nature.

Once the war was over, the world celebrated in color. The 1950s created colors such as salmon, seafoam, and hot pink. New fabrics, such as rayon and nylon, entered the market, and while dyes were still not very good, they provided just the right sheen to go with pale woods and plastics. Furniture began to come in "styles"—Spanish, Mediterranean, or French—and fabrics and colors were needed to match. Scandinavian design created a new sense of modern form, abstraction in fabric design, and colors were developed that matched this new spirit.

The social upheaval of the 1960s combined with the Space Age to bring about a revolution not only in political and scientific terms but also in terms of color. The decade began with the stern, dense, crisp International Style, then exploded with color midway through. Fluorescent colors, black light, orange, lime, and lemon yellow were strewn riotously on anything that could make a statement. Psychedelic patterns prevailed. Furniture forms reflected the race to the moon.

In the 1970s technological advances caught up with design innovations. Breakthroughs in the science of paints and pigments made almost any color economically viable. Technology now permitted exploration on a grand scale. Forms with references to the past were given new meaning with color. The development of new colors allowed juxtapositions of colors that could not have been made before. Design and craftsmanship rose to new heights.

The current decade has brought about a synthesis of form and color, combining Bauhaus traditions with a new psychology of color. Colors are constantly being reinvented and put into new contexts—a process of looking backward and forward at the same time. The current generation might not remember the old context, so these colors are surprising and exciting. Each person can have an individual color palette as well as colors that provide personal metaphors. The influences of the media, computer sciences, and technology provide unlimited choices of what to do with personal color preferences. Never before have we had so many possibilities in choosing forms or furnishings and their colors, and never before have we had so many possible creative solutions.

COLORS AND THEIR MEANINGS

Every color has a history and a particular set of meanings. Both physical and emotional characteristics can be linked to any given color, especially the basic spectral colors of red, blue, yellow, and green, as well as black and white.

Red

Red is the color with the longest wavelength, and it is also the warmest hue. Red demands attention and creates excitement. Red objects look closer or larger than they really are. Red is both a bright and a deep color and has been used throughout history as a sacred religious color in many cultures. We also associate red with blood and thus with a primal life force.

Positive red: excitement, apples, richness, royalty, roses, love, sex, valentines, the Red Cross, a red carpet, bishops' robes, red velvet.

Negative red: fire, blood, blushing, the devil, prostitution, adultery, revolution, stop signs, danger.

Blue

Blue is the calming color, based in nature. It is the most flattering color to wear, as well as the most popular car color. Blue is rarely disliked, but it can easily turn from positive to negative (cool to cold).

Positive blue: sky, water, eyes, blue blood, a blue ribbon, bluebells.

Negative blue: a blue mood, depression, blue Mondays, drowning or illness (turning blue), rancid food, once in a blue moon, frost or ice.

Yellow

A strong, bright color, yellow is expansive and stimulating. It has the highest reflective level of all the colors and is generally perceived as being cheerful.

Positive yellow: the sun, serenity, buttercups, butter, cheese, warmth.

Negative yellow: cowardice, fever, jaundice, shame, contempt.

Red is the first color to be noticed in any environment. Photos: Brent K. Smith and Janice Gehlmeyer.

Yellow is a color that is instantly identified. Photo: Brent K. Smith.

Green

Although made from blue and yellow, green has its own set of meanings. It is the most restful color and is often used in institutions as a wall color. Green is associated with nature and tranquility.

Positive green: grass, trees, spring, fertility, freshness, salads, gardens, money.

Negative green: mold/decay, illness, witchcraft, jealousy.

Black

Black absorbs the most light of any color, and is thought of as opaque rather than transparent. A true black is an absence of any color or light, but most blacks must be defined in contrast to their surroundings.

Positive black: night, coal, oil, power, tuxedos, the little black dress, black tie, black cars.

Negative black: night, fear, death, black heart, black masks, blackball, black-hearted, blacklist, blackmail, black cats.

White

White, like black, is only found in nature, in varying degrees of off-white and gray. It is perceived as a "good" color, although in the Orient it is a funeral color. White reflects the most light of any color.

Positive white: purity, angels, nurses, cleanliness, brides, virginity, snow, chalk.

Negative white: ghosts, a death pallor, icebergs, sterility.

COLOR APPLICATIONS

Color is often used for purposes other than decoration or design. Luminescent colors, for example, are used by the highway department for signs and markers, as well as by some fire departments for their trucks. A bright orange serves a practical purpose on life jackets, hunting gear, and bicycle reflectors; it lets people be seen instantly.

Institutional settings are often painted in particular colors, as years of study have shown color to affect personality and behavior. It is well known, for example, that red excites and pale green tranquilizes, making each useful in appropriate spaces. Red is a good color to use for hurrying customers out of a fast-food restaurant. Pale green is often a choice for schools to calm over-energetic students. The following discussion touches briefly on some industry standards for color use.

Health Care Facilities

The best colors to use in hospital or health care settings are warm neutrals and light greens. White, traditionally associated with nursing and health care, is seldom used for wall color. It is very harsh on the eyes, and color rendition in a white environment is poor. Also, a patient looks more sickly in a white gown. Blue walls, however, have a calming effect. When walls are blue, the surroundings expand and one's sense of time is unhurried and tranquil. Green is best for the operating room as it is the complement of red (blood and tissue) and can neutralize the afterimage doctors and nurses experience from concentrating on wounds.

It is thought that alternating soothing colors with touches of more stimulating colors speeds patient recovery. In hospital bedrooms, since the light is generally on the headwall, the headwall should be neutral and the accent color used on the opposite wall. The public areas in a hospital often have touches of bright red or orange to help cheer the atmosphere.

A designer should avoid using yellows and greens in hospital patient areas as they give skin an even more sickly pallor. Stripes are not considered a good idea, as they create too much visual tension. Gray is too cold, and lavender or purple disturbs the eye's focus, producing a yellow-green afterimage. White, as mentioned earlier, has no therapeutic application but tends to signify sterility or purity and so is used often in ancillary facilities.

Penal Institutions

Blues, browns, greens, and earth colors are known to have a soothing effect and are frequently used in a prison environment. Yellow can provide bits of cheer in a classroom or work area. Reds and oranges, however, are too intense and create too much excitement and should be avoided. Yellow-green can be used in a hallway or area to discourage loitering.

Schools

While a murky, pale green is thought of as a traditional school-wall color, it is actually better to use some of the brighter, warmer colors. Yellow is known to improve the attentiveness of children and red to stimulate activity. Touches of these bright colors add cheerfulness and encourage participation.

Food Service Areas

Elegant restaurants use colors that are flattering to the human complexion. A good choice would be pink lights designed to shine on warm neutrals or earth colors. On the other hand, in a fast-food area stimulating colors encourage rapid eating. In either case blue should be avoided because it distorts the appearance of red meat.

Retail Stores

The colors in a store depend in large part on the merchandise being displayed. Reds, oranges, and yellows are attention grabbing, dynamic, and cheerful. Greens, browns, and earth tones suggest tradition, elegance, and comfort, but care must be taken to avoid the space turning dull or sad looking.

Color is also used in retail environments for store identification, as a theme that can be carried through the design of the space into the graphics of logos and shopping bags. These are often stronger chromes, which create energy as well as provide a signature.

Offices

Earth colors are reassuring in an office environment, and greens are calming. But yellow is known to improve work attentiveness and create a cheerful atmosphere. White gives off too much glare in a workspace. Blue, although calming, can also make employees feel cold and distant. Maroon or deep green used as accents are associated with dignity and power, especially in reception or executive areas.

Executive status frequently is expressed through the use of natural materials—rich woods, marbles, and stone. In the offices of lower-level employees, an increased use of color as well as of man-made materials such as laminates and painted surfaces can be found.

In industrial areas color can be used to give a sense of place, either to break up a large space into smaller units, or to identify position on an assembly line. Color coding to designate different storage or work areas can be more effective than words. High-stress environments need a calming atmosphere, which is easily achieved through color. When workers must use their eyes a great deal, it helps to use low-reflective colors, such as "eye-ease" green. Flat, absorptive colors can ease the strain of working at computer terminals all day.

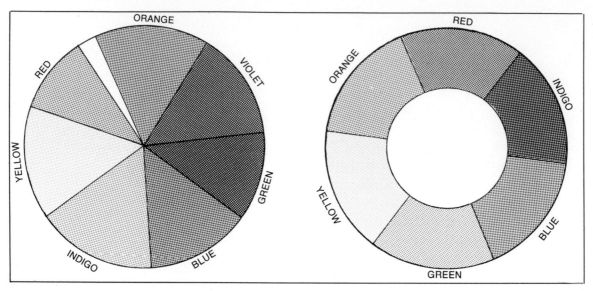

Newton's color wheel.   Goethe's color wheel.

COLOR CLASSIFICATIONS AND SYSTEMS

Efforts to arrange colors in logical sequences have existed since the 1600s. However, the task has proved difficult and complex. The range of colors between the basic colors of the spectrum is practically infinite, yet some degree of naming and classification must be attempted for those who use color as a working tool. Colors need names beyond their spectral red-yellow-green-blue-violet categories. Numbering each color serves a sequential purpose but does not indicate any color characteristics.

The Color Wheel

Sir Isaac Newton was the first to attempt to arrange colors into a logical sequence in the early 1700s by providing the first color wheel (in which spectral colors are arranged around a circle). It was found that only three basic colors were needed to produce white light: red, green, and blue. These colors make up what is called the additive, or spectral, primary colors. When dealing with pig-

ment, however, the primary colors must be shifted slightly to red, blue, and yellow, or those colors that cannot be obtained by mixtures of other colors. In either case the primary colors stand in the corners of an equilateral triangle placed within the color wheel circle, and they mix to produce all other colors. Secondary colors are those made up of any two primaries (orange, for example). Tertiary colors are made of one secondary color plus more of one of that color's primaries (blue-violet, for example).

A century after Newton's color discoveries, Goethe published a massive book on color theory. In addition, many attempts were made to translate the essentially two-dimensional color wheel into three dimensions. In 1772 Johann Lambert developed a color pyramid. Red, yellow, and blue were positioned at the corners of the base, surmounted by seven levels of mixed shades that became progressively lighter toward the top, finally reaching white. Various other scientists created color spheres, cubes, and geometric shapes.

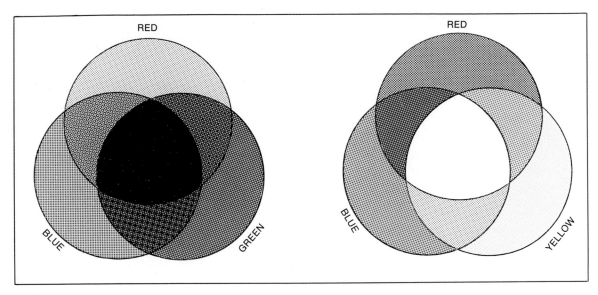

The additive primary colors.

The subtractive primary colors.

Naming Colors

There are various ways to name colors, each with its own set of limitations. The easiest, and most limited, is to use the name of the underlying hue, plus an indication of the color's dominant theme—bluish-red, for example. It is also common to use a qualifying adjective with a color, as in pale blue. These names offer some indication of what the color might look like but are very unspecific.

The most common way of naming colors is to provide a romantic title, but this often indicates little about the color beyond a broad category. Romantic names are often based on nature, flowers, fruits, or gemstones, or on some emotional state, as in passion pink.

Painters' pigments also provide color names, such as ultramarine or yellow ochre. These names are most often based on the color's chemical composition. And finally, many attempts have been made to identify colors with numerical systems.

Today, color naming is big business for the fashion and retail industries. What might have been popular fifteen years ago as

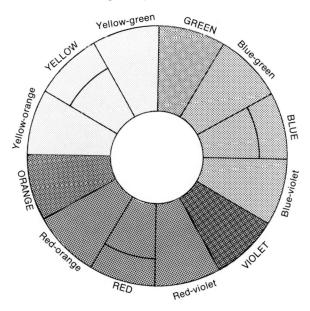

The basic color wheel.

mint green can be newly marketable as pale malachite. We have the technology to produce an infinite number of tints or shades of a color, but paint and dye manufacturers must narrow their selection for a particular year to relatively few. Color consultants work hard to determine, each season, which new colors will find their way into the marketplace.

Color Classifications

Most contemporary color systems classify colors according to hue, saturation, and lightness or by black-and-white content. A. H. Munsell first published in 1929 a volume of color specifications, which has since been updated and still serves as a widely used guide to color. Notations are given for over 1,000 colors, designating hue, value, and chrome in an initial-and-number format.

A system recently developed specifically for use by architects and designers is the PANTONE®* Professional Color System. This matching system features a range of 1,001 opaque colors, each chosen to be of optimal use in the design field. Each color is given a name (translated into six languages)

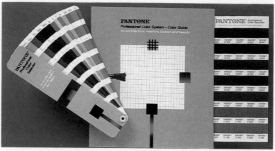

The PANTONE®* Professional Color System. (* Pantone, Inc.'s check-standard ı trademark for color reproduction and color reproduction materials.)

and a number that indicates lightness, hue, and saturation in a general way. A specifier, containing tear-out color chips, coordinates with a fan-out color selector, and the system is geared for use in all mediums, including fabrics, ceramics, paints, carpets, and plastics.

COLOR RULES AND COLOR SCHEMES

Rules and guidelines for using color exist in everything from how to paint a painting to how to decorate a bedroom too how to pick a wardrobe. As with all rules, color rules are meant to be broken by the artistic innovators of the day. Then new "rules" will be written based on these new discoveries. The public response to the new is often one of dismay or outrage, at least until the concept is incorporated into mass culture.

But to an extent, color rules and traditional color schemes can facilitate making color choices, whether it be for a small chair or for a whole building. Some rules are based in physical reality; how colors respond to one another. Other rules are dictated by technological limitations or materials. Still others are based on the experience of designers.

The Physical Rules

There are many tried and true ways to use color in space, based on how colors contrast with or enhance one another, how color temperatures are juxtaposed, and how well our eyes are willing to accept optical tricks. The statements that follow are a few of the most common observations about decorative color.

Colors look stronger in large areas than in small areas. Therefore, the larger the space, the lighter or more neutral the color should be. Brightness increases as surface size decreases.

Colors are affected by their adjoining colors. A medium-toned color looks darker against a light color than against a dark color. The reverse also holds true.

Warm colors are more suitable for rooms with northern exposures, as they simulate sunshine; cool colors counteract the warmth of a sun-filled room.

Light colors make small rooms look

A traditional interior.

larger; dark colors make large rooms look smaller.

Simple colors are recommended on elaborate forms, and vice versa.

Color Schemes

Design professionals traditionally have used formulas for choosing colors for a fabric, a room, or even for use throughout an entire building. These traditional color schemes coordinate with the basic color wheel.

Simple monochromatic: A single hue, along with its tonal variations (tints and shades).

Complex monochromatic: A single hue used with black and white. The neutral is often used to contrast with the hue and bring out architectural detail.

Simple complementary: Two colors used together that are exactly opposite on the color wheel (bichromatic).

Complex complementary: Two complementary colors both tinged with a third hue. For example, red and blue, each tinged with yellow, makes the two colors more harmonious.

Color can be used to change our perceptions of exterior space. The "windows" of the building are an optical illusion—painted on. Photo: Brent K. Smith.

Chapter 4

THE SYSTEM OF COLOR

This section will take the physical realities of color and show how they can be translated into real space. To do so it is necessary to define a common framework or vocabulary that can be used to talk about specific color applications. The use of color can be broken down into six elements: definition, progression, emotion, aesthetics, manipulation, and dimension.

Definition essentially fixes the limits or boundaries of an object in space.

Progression tells us how to move in a space, either literally or visually. It provides sequence or succession for a space.

Emotion attacks the senses, providing strong feelings or causing strong reactions to color in a space.

Aesthetics uses light and color to elicit a response based in history or creative sources.

Manipulation modifies the perception of a form or space to suit a particular purpose.

Dimension defines the locus of an object or space in terms of adjacent objects or surroundings. It establishes relative size and importance.

Viewed as a totality, these elements provide a logic or discipline for using light and color to modify or alter our environment.

COLOR AND DEFINITION

Color has the ability to define; it is one of the elements that allows the eye to precisely identify the shape of a form and the position of an object. While light and shadow provide a great deal of information about a three-dimensional object, color completes the image, giving the form a more precise shape as well as expressive impact. If an object has color, then its shadows also will have color —hence, the effects of a particular color can go far beyond its simple application on a surface. The more complex the relationships between forms and shadows, the more color must be given careful consideration.

Understanding color as a defining element is the first step in seeing how color can be

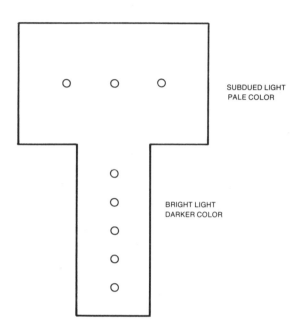

SUBDUED LIGHT
PALE COLOR

BRIGHT LIGHT
DARKER COLOR

Color can influence progression through a space.

a conference room or add spirit and fun in a school or other child-oriented environment.

When the concepts of using warm and cool colors with either two-dimensional or three-dimensional progression are com-tion, or continue. Light, too, can be used to highlight space, by itself or in conjunction with color. In a restaurant, for example, areas designated for a particular waiter are often subtly defined by color changes. Light and/or color might be used for focus on a buffet area or display.

Color also can create the illusion of move-ment in a two-dimensional situation. A flat, rectangular wall can be made to look like a curving wall, either concave or convex. The color on the wall simply must move from light to dark and back again. Optically, the gradations will cause the surface to either move forward or recede. This can add dra-matic effects to a plain wall in a hallway or

bined, the possibilities start to multiply. If light and shadow are introduced into the equation, perspective can be created. A nar-row hallway can be made to look as if it is curving, or a ceiling can be made to seem arched or shaped. The addition of a paint-erly or architectural illusion produces *trompe l'oeil*—a wall becomes a meadow or a hall-way gains a window with a view.

The most important thing to remember is that light and color must always be kept in balance.

Color increases the sense of progression as the eye travels up the surface of this office building. Photo: Brent K. Smith.

Light and color lead the eye and encourage physical progression toward the food service area.
Design: the Miller Organization, New York City.

COLORS AND EMOTION

Color elicits response. This response can occur on many levels, both physical and cultural. We begin with the physical recognition of color in the form of the information contained in light as it travels from the optic nerves to the brain. To this we add on all the cultural responses we have to color, learned from history and from using color in our own lives. Finally, we consider current styles or trends, which affect not only our perceptions of color but also the way we dress and the contents of our homes.

Color preference is largely a cultural phenomenon, whereas color response is a combination of reactions to physical phenomena and cultural associations. Both together af-

fect how we feel about color and how we use it.

There are documented physical responses to both light and color that can be separated from learned responses. Studies have shown that humans have a direct reaction to light levels, becoming depressed in the winter or in northern climates where there is little bright light. Workers on a night shift need more light to compensate for the lack of natural daylight. (For an in-depth look at the physical and emotional effects of color, we suggest the recently published *Wagner Color Response Report*, Color Communications, Inc., Chicago.) At full intensity, the level of stimulation a color generates can be cor-

our homes. Yet we rely on safe, predetermined choices, because we do not know how to formulate color ideas of our own.

Culture give us color associations that are comfortable and reassuring because of their familiarity. *Style* give us color choices dictated by the trends of the moment in fashion and art. *Design,* finally, provides color choices based on the contrast between non-specific colors for particular effects. All three elements combine to formulate our aesthetic taste.

As a cultural phenomenon, the metaphors behind color can evoke certain periods in history or particular nationalities. A specific red instantly will tell us of its Oriental origins. Wedgewood blue comes packed with associations.

The style of color is dictated by the fashion industry, fabric manufacturers, and the art and design world.

Design professionals use formulas for choosing the colors in a print fabric, in a room, or even throughout a whole building. A simple analogous color scheme, for example, uses a single color as a main theme, then uses that color's various tints and shades as accents.

Decoration involves the relationship between particular hues. Design, however, concentrates on the contrasts between non-

specific colors. Red placed against mauve, blue against black, all begin to change form. The less specific a color, the more it approaches design and the stronger the focus on what the color does to the space rather than on what particular color it is. Color used as a design element can push/pull, accentuate, erase, darken/lighten, and evoke.

Color is only new when it is given a new relationship. It can then become fresh again, both to the color palette and to the form on which it is applied.

COLOR AND MANIPULATION

Color can convince us to see a different reality. It can manipulate in both physical and mental ways.

Each color brings with it a vast array of associations that tell us how we will respond to that color, both in and out of context. An orange is orange. If, one day, you went into the supermarket and the oranges were mauve, the effect would be most unsettling.

You would probably not buy those oranges, even if they tasted exactly the same. That is a simplified example of how color can mentally manipulate.

Color can also manipulate our perception of space. It is possible to recreate a historical setting without actually using historic materials. The Victorian era can be recreated by using deep reds and hunter green. The

Warm and cool colors manipulate the eye. Photos:
Ruth Amiel.

Actual applications of color can be real or unreal, as seen in this *trompe l'oeil* mural. Designers: Evergreene P.S., Inc., New York City. Photo: Jeff Greene.

Chapter 5

SOLUTIONS

The following case studies will show how using color far transcends the application of paint to a surface. Color manipulates both two- and three-dimensional conditions, affecting size, shape, emotions, and times.

Using the vocabulary provided in the previous section—definition, progression, emotion, aesthetics, manipulation, and dimension—these studies will analyze using color in a variety of situations from historic to modern, from modest to ambitious.

It is important, however, to keep in mind that all these aspects of color are interrelated. In an actual project, it is rare that one single color effect will stand alone, even though some initially may be more obvious than others. In reality, the more these elements combine, the more color approaches design.

ENVIRONMENTAL COLOR

Fallingwater, the Frank Lloyd Wright house commissioned in the 1950s is the epitome of a house built to nature's specifications and colored by the changing seasons. To view the house from the exterior, although the necessary modifications of shelter (walls, a roof, and so on) are clear, little seems to create a barrier between the interior and exterior landscape.

Architecturally, the house is cantilevered out over the stone site. The materials and finishes used to construct the building echo those of the surroundings, but the strong geometry is softened by foliage and by the abundant use of natural light. Visually, it is hard to tell where nature ends and the house begins.

Definition

Both scale and color are defined by the natural surroundings of the house. The contemporary hard lines of the architecture melt away as the natural exterior textures blend with the trees. Boundaries between house and landscape are not quite certain. The colors of the trees, rocks, and water found outside reflect on the glass walls and windows

fect of being in this house, however, is far from intimidating or unfriendly. The scale is quite human, thanks to the use of small patterns and colors based in nature. It unquestionably reflects the love of nature of both owner and designer.

PRE-EXISTING COLOR

The idea of using a glass box as an architectural form creates a space that is both defined and contained by its surroundings. Whatever shape the house might have disappears. Whatever colors the space might be given already exist. Philip Johnson's Connecticut guest house is such a glass box, and it provides a visual statement of impeccable understatement. In the same way as its pristine shape makes it "invisible" against its surroundings, its color is provided by the changing seasonal landscape.

Guesthouse. Architect: Philip Johnson. Photo: Richard Payne.

Definition

While the edges of the glass box remind the viewer that the structure is really a geometric form, they are also thin enough so that the form is easily ignored. The illusion, therefore, is one of "non-form." The awareness of shape comes second, after the awareness of transparency. This is also a house without any applied color. Edges and supports blend with the tree trunks in the background. Definition, therefore, is minimal—sufficient only to provide environmental comfort.

Emotion

The viewer is clearly aware that this structure is man-made. Its materials—mainly metal and glass—do not pretend to be anything else and are not the same as those of the surrounding environment, such as wood or stone, which might make the structure blend in to the outdoors. Emotional response is predicated by the "color" of the day, just as if one were spending the day outside. The sense of enclosure or shelter is minimal, leaving little interference between viewer and nature.

Aesthetics

Because the glass box is surrounded by undulating trees and distant hills, even though the lines of the house are straight, the glass picks up the hues and reflections of nature, and the shape becomes uncertain. Color in this case, like the form, is a strict, intellectual idea. It exists as and changes with whatever else might be around or inside the box.

Manipulation

A house made of glass creates striking, cold values that contrast with the warmth of the

Awnings protrude, doorways recede. Visual progression also occurs from one store to the next and along the length of the fire escape. We assume a transition between interior and exterior. We also perceive real perspective.

Emotion

The emotion surrounding these stores is nostalgic and warm. The colors used support the emotion. These are period colors, undesigned but personal and inviting. They reach back for a remembrance of a time past.

Aesthetics

The colors used to decorate the storefronts evoke the popular and available colors of the period during which the buildings were constructed. The *trompe l'oeil* suggests the passage of time. The paints appear worn, the materials well used. Color first creates the picture, but it also affects the form.

Manipulation

The illusion of space is made by contrasting warm and cool colors. This constant "push-pull" plays a visual game that heightens the *trompe l'oeil* effects. The manipulation, however, is also one of emotion. We are pulled back to a previous era, invited to believe that this neighborhood still exists. The use of stage-set colors in period tones is crucial to the emotional effect.

Dimension

Depth is created by illusion and association. The windows and doorways all feel real. The scale is correct, making the real and unreal elements work together as a cohesive whole.

COLOR AS DISGUISE

A dry cleaning store has little intrinsic glamour, but this example, through color, effect, and a sense of humor, is both intriguing and playful.

The front window tantalizes: the colorful graphics cover up just enough of what is inside so that it is not clear to the passerby. The visitor who steps closer can see not only into the customer area but also through to the industrial equipment.

Once inside, a maximum of effect occurs with a minimum of materials—a mixture of industrial standards, modernist details, and whimsy, such as the timeless park bench. The machinery in the back, which ordinarily would be intimidating, is now simply part of the game explored by the geometrics of the space—the shock of the bright dropped ceiling grid, the strong diagonal splitting the counter area in two.

Definition

Color is part of how this vast space is contained. It provides visual limits, cutting the space into manageable segments and echoing the traffic and work patterns.

PASSIVE COLOR

This suburban operations center for a brokerage company is designed to quiet the frenetic activity that occurs during each working day. Color, much more than design, tranquilizes the space and provides an ordered, calming atmosphere. The materials used are soft-finish, heathery tones that absorb rather than reflect. One particular color, along with variations in the same family, give a color theme to each floor. The colors—soft blues and mauves—are almost neutral. These offices can be occupied for long periods of time without visual fatigue. In addition, the colors homogenize the diverse group of people, giving a sense of belonging to the company. The resulting space is rather anonymous. Even though the individual work areas are clustered instead of placed in long rows, the effect is the same: a calm, unified, neutral work environment.

Definition

Color does not define in this project. It indicates neither status nor job function. It homogenizes rather than separates.

Progression

Use of soft, muted hues with few contrasts produces a sense of a slowed pace. The eye is not led in particular directions, but instead relaxes. The work areas can be inhabited for many hours without strain or anxiety. Only in the cafeteria is life hurried up a bit, and there it is done with reflective surfaces (a polished stainless-steel ceiling) that create some energy and sparkle.

Aesthetics

This office landscape unifies hundreds of people with different personalities and jobs. Even the executive office reflects egalitarian design and uses the same color harmonies found in the other work areas. The furnishings might be expensive or antique, but the overall effect is that the colors establish the executive's link to the rest of the staff.

Manipulation

The single-color theme pleases the eye, quiets, and promotes the feeling of "team effort." Without drama, the spaces are long-term and comfortable, with much more thought given design rather than style. The tranquil interiors are offset by the surrounding landscape. The changing colors of nature provide a touch of vivid accent in a background of matte heathers and soft edges.

Dimension

The colors delineate floors, but not interior spaces. Various shades of the same hue are used for the walls, floors, chairs, and partitions. A neutral gray covers the laminated surfaces, providing little contrast. The colors themselves are hues made up of many close shades that result in a comfortable environment. The colors could easily be interchanged from floor to floor and could be either warm or cool without changing the overall effect.

Brokerage company operations center. Design: the Miller Organization, New York City. Photos: James D'Addio.

SOLUTIONS

Aesthetics

Daylight yields a clean sweep of space with clearly defined postmodernist edges that is still neutral against the merchandise being sold. Night colors are richer, heightened. Shoppers become aware of the color rather than the shapes. Color becomes much more visually demanding, less passive.

Manipulation

The forms are strong, interesting, and the viewer is aware of their weight. In the daylight, the softness of the colors makes the forms recede into the background, allowing the eye to focus on the retail goods. By night the forms are accentuated. The stores and merchandise fall away against the drama of the stronger colors and shapes.

Dimension

The sense of scale changes dramatically from day to night. Lack of contrast yields vast space. Contrast provides a sense of enclosure. The walls, ceiling, and details all have much stronger impact through the contrasting evening colors.

COLOR AS BACKGROUND

One effective color detail can take what is essentially a neutral space and turn it into a soft but dramatic background for dining. The theme here is quiet, comfortable, unrushed, and essentially Mediterranean. The *trompe l'oeil* mural transports the viewer to another time and place. The neutral colors support the soft theme. But the color/light detail at the top of each column gives this traditional environment a new twist. The ceiling now becomes reminiscent of a summer sunset sky, floating in space.

The color finishes each column like a traditional decorative capital, but with an unexpected difference that heightens the contrast between old and new, providing an interesting backdrop for good food and relaxation.

Canastels, New York City. Architect/Designer: Charles Morris Mount, Inc., New York City. Photos: Peter Paige Associates, NJ.

Definition

Color occurs on the ceiling and floor but is neutral on the vertical planes in between. This provides a sense of open and extensive space.

Progression

The floor tiles are patterned to give an indication of progression through the space, but essentially this is an area with few edges and therefore few visual limits. The *trompe l'oeil,* too, explodes the room's dimensions.

Emotion

The effect here is one of quiet repose. No one will be hurried in or out. The colors are soft; the lighting warm and even. Few contrasts interfere.

Aesthetics

The use of color here is one of good taste, of timeless culture. It will not soon become dated.

Manipulation

The light/color above each column causes the eye to move beyond the ceiling structure. The mural moves the eye beyond the walls. There is little sense of enclosure.

Dimension

Color brings all the elements of this restaurant together to give a sense of earthiness. The tile floor projects sand, terra firma, and soft stone; the ceiling becomes warm evening light; and in between are soft breezes.

POP CULTURE AND COLOR

The American Café is as much of an all-American story as its location in Washington, D.C. Variations of red, white, and blue combine with jazzy tile patterns to create a fresh, upscale collage of color and texture and a sense of fast movement from spot to spot within the restaurant/bar/gourmet shop.

Definition

Separate colors define the various display areas and provide a circulation pattern. The colors are flat and dense, receding into the background in order to highlight the food.

Progression

It is easy to follow along the route in this space. The articulated ceiling line pulls the eye right through. The floor tiles echo the path.

Emotion

Textures, patterns, colors, all superimposed on one another, create a kinetic space that is full of visual surprises, yet all of the visual activity enhances the function.

Aesthetics

With a changed color palette, this restaurant would be equally at home in California. But the color indicates exactly where it is located. The look is pop culture, done with flag-waving good humor.

Manipulation

There is little regularity to the forms or colors. The entire space plays games with the senses in a young and vital way.

Dimension

The intense, flat colors and the textures provide definite limits to the various areas.

The American Café, Washington, D.C. Architect/Designer: Charles Morris Mount, Inc., New York City. Photos: H. Durstan Saylor.

INDEX

DATE